Basic English for Architecture
—Reading & Writing—

建築を学ぶ人のための総合英語
—リーディング＆ライティング—

Emiko Hirose Horton
Cecilia Smith Fujishima
Masa Horikawa Tsuneyasu
Hanako Kamiya
Justin Pannell
Reina Hirose Horton

NAN'UN-DO

Basic English for Architecture
—Reading & Writing—

Copyright© 2019

by
Emiko Hirose Horton
Cecilia Smith Fujishima
Masa Horikawa Tsuneyasu
Hanako Kamiya
Justin Pannell
Reina Hirose Horton

All Rights Reserved
No part of this book may be reproduced in any form without written permission from the authors and Nan'un-do Co., Ltd.

このテキストの音声を無料で視聴（ストリーミング）・ダウンロードできます。自習用音声としてご活用ください。
以下のサイトにアクセスしてテキスト番号で検索してください。

https://nanun-do.com　テキスト番号 [511945]

※ 無線 LAN（WiFi）に接続してのご利用を推奨いたします。
※ 音声ダウンロードは Zip ファイルでの提供になります。
　お使いの機器によっては別途ソフトウェア（アプリケーション）の導入が必要となります。

Basic English for Architecture <Reading &Writing> 音声ダウンロードページは左記の QR コードからもご利用になれます。

はしがき

　グローバル化が進む中、それぞれの分野においての英語運用能力が求められており、ESP（English for Specific Purposes）の重要性と必要性が認められています。しかし、実際に専門分野に関連した内容のリーディング教材を通した語彙強化や、その分野に関連する内容でのライティング練習に特化した英語テキストは多くはありません。EGP（English for General Purposes）・EAP（English for Academic Purposes）として作成されたテキストは、その目的から非常に広い範囲のトピックを含んでいます。しかし、限られた学習時間の中で建築関連学習や仕事において「使える英語」の力をつけるためには、その分野に特化した語彙を強化し、コミュニケーション力をつけるための学習が必要となります。

　本書は Basic English for Architecture: Listening and Speaking に続き、建築系を学ぶ、あるいは建築系の仕事に携わり始めた学習者のために開発された語学(英語)学習テキストです。Basic English for Architecture: Listening and Speaking と同様の建築に関連するテーマに基づいた Reading Section と Writing Section からなる 12 ユニットで構成されています。

　Reading Section では、様々なトピックを扱ったパッセージを通して、基本的な建築関連の語彙の強化と読解力を養います。Writing Section では、基本的なパラグラフの書き方から最終的には複数のパラグラフで構成された essay が書けるように、段階的にライティングの力をつけていきます。

　学習者のターゲットとしては TOEIC400 点〜550 点レベルを設定しています。建築関連企業でも新入社員の英語力は課題の一つとなっているという声も聞こえてきます。本書は、建築系の大学生および企業における語学研修で使える入門レベルの建築系英語テキストを目指しました。

各ユニットは、以下のように構成されています。

Reading Section:
- 各ユニットのテーマに関連する 500 ワード前後の Reading Passage
- 本文に使用されている Vocabulary の意味
- 単語ベース・文章ベースの問題で語彙力を高める Vocabulary Exercise
- Reading Passage の読解問題

Writing Section:
- パラグラフの書き方を基礎から学ぶ Writing Focus
- Model Paragraph を使った Writing Focus 内容の理解確認
- Model Paragraph を参考にしたライティング応用練習

　本書の作成にあたり、芝浦工業大学建築学部の多くの先生方のご協力とご助言をいただきました。また、伊藤洋子教授（Unit 6）、隈澤文俊教授（Unit 4）、志村秀明教授（Unit 2）、古谷浩教授（Unit 7）には日本語原案を作成いただき、本書のクオリティを高めることができました。皆様に感謝申し上げます。

CONTENTS

Unit 1
Introduction — 6

Unit 2
Planning — 10

Unit 3
Floor Plan — 14

Unit 4
Building Structure — 18

Unit 5
Kitchen — 22

Unit 6
Living Room — 26

Unit 7
    Design Styles   30

Unit 8
    Scales and Dimensions   34

Unit 9
    Colors   38

Unit 10
    Sustainable Design   42

Unit 11
    Natural Hazards   46

Unit 12
    Urban Design   50

Unit 1
Introduction

READING SECTION

What Is Architecture?

If we look in the dictionary for a definition of *architecture*, we find something like architecture is 1) the process of planning, designing, and constructing buildings and other physical structures and 2) the product of this process. In other words,
5 architecture means both the buildings themselves and the process that occurs to build the buildings. But is architecture more than that?

If we examine the contents of an architecture course at a university, our understanding of architecture becomes more complex than the dictionary definition. We can learn more about what architecture is. Looking at the viewpoints of people who design architecture courses, we can see
10 that architecture is a highly integrated and multi-dimensional creative process. Architecture schools combine a variety of different elements—aesthetic, technical, social and environmental—to make a whole. We also learn that architecture doesn't exist in isolation.

When we listen to architects, we can get a better sense of the meaning of architecture and our understanding deepens again. We can see that architecture is not just physical; it is also philosophical
15 and connected to society. For example, the French architect Le Corbusier (1887-1965) believed that a house was a 'machine to live in'; it should be modern and convenient. He thought architecture should use the technological advances in society. Le Corbusier also saw a social role for architecture in raising the quality of life for the working classes. Odile Decq, a contemporary French architect, also emphasizes the philosophical interconnection between architecture and society. From her point
20 of view, to contribute to society, architects need a "deep cultural, sociological, economical, political and ethical understanding of the world."

Toyo Ito, who won the Pritzker Prize in 2011, emphasizes different aspects of architecture. Ito believes that architecture is a way to create order in a world that is always changing. In his work, he wants to bring architecture closer to nature and the local community. His philosophy has influenced
25 Kazuyo Sejima's and Ryue Nishizawa's architecture. Like Ito, they also emphasize 'openness.' In their Pritzker Prize acceptance speech in 2010 they talked about building the Kanazawa Art Museum. They designed it so that people would feel comfortable coming into the building even if they didn't know anything about art.

Although different architects have different views, there are similarities, as they consider the
30 meaning of architecture for both people and the environment. In your studies you will have many opportunities to learn, discover, and deepen your understanding of architecture. You will meet different philosophies and look at architecture from a variety of points of view. As you study and in your daily life, pay attention to the environment around you and the effect that it has on people, and reflect on what architecture means to you.　(455 words)

Vocabulary

definition（定義）, process（過程）, physical（物理的）, complex（複雑な）, viewpoint（見方、観点）, integrated（統合された、総合的な）, multi-dimensional（多次元の）, element（要素）, aesthetic（審美的）, isolation（隔離）, deepen（深める）, quality of life（生活の質）, contemporary（現代の）, philosophical（哲学の）, community（コミュニティ、地域社会）, emphasize（強調する）, consider（考える、考慮する）, reflect（反映する）

Vocabulary Exercise

1 Find the closest meaning from a-e for each word below.

1. isolation (　)
2. definition (　)
3. viewpoint (　)
4. aesthetic (　)
5. reflect (　)

a. appreciation of beauty
b. a way of looking at or thinking about something
c. separated from other persons or things
d. an explanation of the meaning of the word
e. think over

2 Write the most appropriate word to complete the sentences. (You may need to change the form of the word). There are some words in the box that you don't use.

1. Architects (　　　　　) the lifestyle of residents when designing a house.
2. He is quite (　　　　　) and always thinking about the meaning of life.
3. You can (　　　　　) your knowledge of architecture by reading widely.
4. She (　　　　　) the importance of design over function.

| physical | emphasize | philosophical | consider | elements | deepen |

Comprehension Questions

1 Write T if the statement is true according to the text and F if it is not true.

1. According to the dictionary definition, the word "architecture" has two meanings. (　)
2. Philosophy is important in architecture. (　)
3. Toyo Ito designed the Kanazawa Art Museum. (　)
4. Ito's belief about architecture is to use the technological possibilities of the day. (　)
5. Sejima, Nishizawa, and Ito emphasize the importance of 'openness.' (　)

2 Write an answer to each question below.

1. What two aspects does the dictionary definition of architecture include?

   _____.

2. What elements are found in an architectural course?

   _____.

3. What social role did Le Corbusier believe that architecture has?

   _____.

4. What advice does the text give to you as a student?

   _____.

WRITING SECTION

WRITING FOCUS: The Organization of a Paragraph

What is a paragraph?
A paragraph is a group of sentences focusing on one main idea. The main idea is expressed in a sentence that is called a topic sentence at or near the beginning of the paragraph. The topic sentence is usually followed by supporting sentences. Supporting sentences provide details, such as examples, explanations, statistics, and experts' opinions.

Seven basic rules for writing a paragraph
When you are writing a paragraph/paragraphs, pay attention to the following points.
1. Have a topic sentence.
2. Have relevant supporting sentences.
3. Indent the first sentence of the paragraph.
4. Do not start each sentence on a new line.
5. Keep margins on both sides. (If using a word processor, use justification（両端揃え）, or leave about an inch space on both sides if writing by hand.)
6. Use a capital letter at the beginning of each sentence.
7. Use a period, question mark, or exclamation point at the end of each sentence.

Exercise

1 Read the model paragraph and answer the questions.

A MODEL PARAGRAPH

Why I'm studying architecture

My junior high school trip to Kyoto inspired me to become an architect. We visited many famous temples and shrines, including Kinkaku-ji, Ginkaku-ji, and Fushimi Inari. While these temples and shrines were impressive, I was more attracted to Kyoto's narrow and long houses called "machiya." Since I was inspired by the shrines, temples, and machiya, I became very interested in different types of houses. Since then, looking at books and magazines of house design has become one of my hobbies. now, I'm studying architecture at my university and finding out that architecture means much more than simply designing houses. The more I know about architecture, the stronger my desire becomes to study all aspects of architecture
(116 words)

1. Write the topic sentence of the model paragraph.

2 Identify the following supporting sentences and match them using the choices in the box. You may not need to use all of the choices.

1. Since I was inspired by the shrines, temples, and machiya, I became very interested in different types of houses. (   )

2. For example, I visited Kinkaku-ji Temple, Ginkaku-ji Temple, and Fushimi Inari shrine. (   )

3. While these temples and shrines were impressive, I was more attracted to Kyoto's narrow and long houses called "machiya." (   )

> examples   explanations   statistics   expert's opinion

3 Read the model paragraph again and put a check mark (✔) if the following rules are satisfied.

Rule 3: (   ) Indent the first sentence of the paragraph.
Rule 4: (   ) Do NOT start each sentence on a new line.
Rule 5: (   ) Keep margins on both side. (If using word a processor, use justification, or leave about an inch space on both sides if writing by hand.)
Rule 6: (   ) Use a capital letter at the beginning of a sentence.
Rule 7: (   ) Use a period at the end of each sentence.

Unit 2
Planning

READING SECTION

Monja Street in Tsukishima

Nishinaka-dori used to be a lively shopping street in Tsukishima in eastern Tokyo. Now, if you go there, instead of a shopping street lined with retail stores, you'll find an area that has become famous for its dozens of *monja* restaurants. *Monja* is a Tokyo-style of
5 *okonomiyaki*. It is made with a thin batter of flour and *dashi* and finely chopped cabbage which is pan-fried at your table. Depending on people's taste, it is mixed with other ingredients, such as fish roe, meat, and even strawberries and cream.

Tsukishima is an island in Tokyo Bay made from land reclaimed during the Meiji era. Reclamation was completed in 1892 and it became a site for factories that were needed for Japan's industrialization.
10 A ferry service began the same year, and the number of people moving into Tsukishima grew rapidly. In those days, many workers from the Ishikawajima shipyard (now IHI) and related factories, such as Ishii Tekkosho (now Ishii Iron Works Co., Ltd) and Tsukishima Kikai (now Tsukishima Kikai Co., Ltd), moved into the area. Shops and street stalls began to appear in the area. Some sites for entertainment, such as a movie theater and a *rakugo* theater, opened and attracted people from outside the area as well.
15 The low prices of goods, targeted at factory workers, brought many people to the town. As a result, people started to open shops, and many merchants from other places opened shops in Tsukishima; the Nishinaka-dori flourished. Tsukishima was the first place in Japan to have a koban. It opened in 1921.

In 1923, the Great Kanto Earthquake destroyed most of Tsukishima. Many buildings were burnt down. After the disaster, the streets were rebuilt in a style known as *kanban-kenchiku*. These kinds of
20 buildings were western style with a shop on the first floor and a residence on the second. The name *kanban* was used because typically the shop had advertising billboards on the outside. Tsukishima had gotten a new look.

Although much of eastern Tokyo was destroyed in the air raids of the Pacific War, Tsukishima received little damage. After the war, the town lost the liveliness of the pre-war era. Factories, which
25 had been producing for the war, began to close down and government control of unauthorized street stalls became tighter. Some of these street stalls were turned into regular shops, and the shopping street gradually revived. The Yurakucho subway line, which started in 1988, gave new life to Tsukishima.

From around that time, the number of *monja* restaurants began to increase. Many existing merchants changed their business to *monja* restaurants, and the town became famous as "Tsukishima
30 *Monja* Town". These days Tsukishima is a lively town with a nostalgic atmosphere which is often featured on television food programs. The shopping street lined with old-town monja shops and narrow alleys between old houses make it a popular destination for people looking to experience traditional Tokyo. (483 words)

(Based on the Japanese passage written by Dr. Hideaki Shimura of Shibaura Institute of Technology)
35 http://www.tsukishima.arc.shibaura-it.ac.jp/ 月島長屋学校

Vocabulary

lively（活気のある）, instead of（〜の代わりに）, retail store（小売店, 商店）, dozens of（何ダースもの, たくさんの）, batter（小麦粉を水で溶いたもの）, finely（細かく）, chopped（切られた, 切ってある）, taste（好み）, ingredient（料理の材料）, fish roe（魚卵）, reclaimed（埋め立てられた）, complete（完成する）, industrialization（工業化, 産業化）, ferry service（フェリー／渡しの運行）, shipyard（造船所）, appear（現れる）, attract（惹きつける）, merchant（商人）, flourish（繁栄する, 繁盛する）, disaster（災難）, rebuilt（再建された）, residence（住居）, billboard（大きな看板）, air raid（空襲）, unauthorized（無許可の）, turn into（〜になる）, revive（再び栄える）, nostalgic（懐かしい）, atmosphere（雰囲気）, alley（路地）, destination（目的地）

Unit 2

Vocabulary Exercise

1 Find the closest meaning from a-e for each word below.

1. attract ( )
2. unauthorized ( )
3. atmosphere ( )
4. alley ( )
5. residence ( )

a. not given official permission
b. a narrow/small street
c. to make someone interested in
d. dwelling place
e. mood of a place

2 Write the most appropriate word to complete the sentences. (You may need to change the form of the word.) There are some words in the box that you don't use.

1. Around Tokyo Bay there are many new towns built on (　　　　) land.
2. The old industrial area has (　　　　) since new condominiums were built.
3. They decided to go out for monja (　　　　) making dinner at home.
4. The old town gives me a (　　　　) feeling.

| instead of | reclaimed | nostalgic | revive | attract | destination |

COMPREHENSION QUESTIONS

1 Write T if the statement is true according to the text and F if it is not true.

1. The main street of Tsukishima is lined with retail shops. ( )
2. The factories of Tsukishima were built on reclaimed land. ( )
3. The Tsukishima area played a part in Japan's industrialization. ( )
4. After the Kanto earthquake, many street stalls opened in Tsukishima. ( )
5. The main transport in Tsukishima is buses and ferries. ( )

2 Write an answer to each question below.

1. What are examples of ingredients that can be added to *monja* as options?

2. What event caused great damage to Tsukishima?

3. What two reasons are given for Tsukishima becoming less lively after the war?

4. In addition to *monja* shops, what attracts visitors to Tsukishima?

WRITING SECTION

WRITING FOCUS: Topic Sentence

The topic sentence states the main idea of a paragraph. It is usually found at or near the beginning of the paragraph. A good topic sentence includes both a **topic** for the paragraph and a **focus point of the topic.** The **topic** tells you what the paragraph is about. The **focus point** tells the purpose of the pragraph (see the example below). The topic sentence provides the reader with the direction of the ideas that will follow. One paragraph has one main topic, and all the sentences that follow the topic sentence should give more information to support the topic sentence. The main idea in the topic sentence is often restated in the **concluding sentence**, which should be the last sentence of the paragraph. Let's look at the topic and topic focus of some topic sentences.

Topic: Tokyo
Focus of the topic: *Places for shopping and eating out*
Topic sentence: Tokyo has many places for shopping and eating out.

Let's look at the body paragraphs in the reading passage *Monja Street in Tsukishima*. (We'll look at the organization of an essay, introduction paragraphs, body paragraphs, and concluding paragraphs in more details in later units.)

- **Topic**: Tsukishima
  Focus of the topic: *made from land reclaimed during the Meiji era*
  Topic sentence: Tsukishima is an island in Tokyo Bay *made from land reclaimed during the Meiji era.*

- **Topic**: The Great Kanto Earthquake
  Focus of the topic: *destroyed most of Tsukishima*
  Topic sentence: In 1923, The Great Kanto Earthquake *destroyed most of Tsukishima.*

- **Topic**: Tsukishima
  Focus of the topic: *received little damage*
  Topic sentence: Although much of eastern Tokyo was destroyed in the air raids of the Pacific War, Tsukishima *received little damage.*

Unit 2

EXERCISE

1 Analyze the model paragraph.

A MODEL PARAGRAPH

Changes in My Hometown

My hometown has changed a lot since I was a child. There used to be a lot of small, family-owned shops on the main street, which gave a warm community feeling, but they shut early in the evening. Nowadays, the convenience stores are not so friendly, but they have most products that I need and are open all through the night. Another change is the type of people. In the past there were a lot of children in the parks, but now most of the people in the parks are old. There are a lot more services for old people too. Recently, the train station had an elevator installed. There are many changes, some good and some not so good, but I still love my hometown. (126 words)

1. Circle the topic sentence of the model paragraph.

   _____

2. Write the topic of the topic sentence.

   _____

3. Write the topic focus of the topic sentence.

   _____

2 Practice writing topic sentences.

1. **Topic:** My Hometown

   Focus of topic: _____

   Topic sentence: _____

2. **Topic:** Architecture

   Focus of topic: _____

   Topic sentence: _____

3. **Topic:** _____ (Something you are interested in.)

   Focus of topic: _____

   Topic sentence: _____

Unit 3
Floor Plan

READING SECTION

Danchi: Changing Lifestyles

    In the years after World War II, the big cities of Japan faced a crisis with a lack of housing. More than one-sixth of the houses in Japan were destroyed in the war. At the same time, the population was increasing due to the post-war baby boom. In addition to the baby boom, there was population movement; many people were returning from overseas and others were moving to the big cities from rural areas. The first priority for the government was improving the economy. After that, the government began to prioritize housing. The formation of the Japan Housing Corporation in 1955 began a large-scale transformation of housing in Japan.

    With the development of *danchi* and apartment living, there was a transformation in the way that Japanese living space was arranged. In the past, *tatami* rooms enabled multi-function spaces. But in the post-war era, there was a shift in thinking; the space for sleeping and eating was separated. Apartment living had a space for sleeping set aside from eating space where food was prepared. This style of living created a new market for western-style furniture as people changed from sitting on the floor to eat to sitting at chairs and tables. According to sociologists, the layout of *danchi* apartments normalized post-war nuclear families. They were too small for married children to continue living with their parents.

    The *danchi* were a symbol of progress and prosperity. The *danchi* had features that were not found in traditional Japanese homes. These included stainless steel sinks, flush toilets and even elevators. People dreamed of living in *danchi*, and applications to live in them flooded in. They were so popular that lotteries were held to allocate places. In 1957, Mainichi Shimbun reported that the odds of being successful in applying for an apartment in the Hikarigaoka Danchi in Kashiwa, Chiba Prefecture, were more than 25,000 to 1.

    As time passed, the *danchi* lost their shine and became less popular. They lacked the cultural liveliness of established towns, and people began to associate them with isolation and loneliness. As young people moved out to start their own lives, the residents left behind grew old. As newer facilities were built in more modern buildings, the popularity of *danchi* began to decrease. As a result, decisions need to be made whether to demolish or renovate old-style buildings.

    In recent years, *danchi* in some areas have started to experience a revival. Renovation companies have recognized that if apartments are to remain they need to be redesigned to fit people's lifestyle. This includes a trend to convert old-style apartments into open plan studios. In some cases companies are removing the interior walls and painting the apartments white, creating a fresh, minimalist aesthetic. The renovated *danchi* are becoming increasingly popular with young couples and singles. The post-war evolution of *danchi* shows that housing changes in response to changes in people's lifestyles. At the same time, the style of housing influences the way that people live. (493 words)

Vocabulary

lack（失う，欠けている），one-sixth（6分の1），priority（優先），prioritize（優先順位をつける），formation（設立，構造），Japan Housing Corporation（日本住宅公団），transformation（改変，変換，変貌，変化），multi-function（多機能），sociologist（社会学者），layout（レイアウト），normalize（標準化する，普通になる），post-war（戦後），nuclear family（核家族），progress and prosperity（進化と繁栄），stainless steel sink（ステンレスの流し），flush toilet（水洗トイレ），application（申し込み），allocate（配分する，振り分ける），odds（可能性，確率），shine（魅力），cultural liveliness（文化的な活気），established town（古くからある町），left behind（取り残される），be built in（備え付けられた），revival（復活，再生），renovation（改修，改築），studio（ワンルーム），minimalist aesthetic（ミニマリストの美学）

Unit 3

Vocabulary Exercise

1 Find the closest meaning from a-e for each word below.

1. normalize ( )
2. allocate ( )
3. shine ( )
4. facility ( )
5. lack ( )

a. insufficient, not enough
b. attractiveness
c. to distribute or assign something
d. something created to serve a particular function
e. to become standard, widely accepted

2 Write the most appropriate word to complete the sentences. (You may need to change the form of the word.) There are some words in the box that you don't use.

1. I prefer a ( ) sink rather than a tiled one.
2. In the past people often lived in multi-generation homes but now ( ) are more common.
3. ( ) furniture cannot be carried out of a room.
4. Please do this task as your first ( ). It has to be finished as soon as possible.

| revival | multi-function | stainless steel | built-in | priority | nuclear family |

Comprehension Questions

1 Write T if the statement is true according to the text and F if it is not true.

1. Japan lacked housing in the 1950s. ( )
2. After the war, providing housing was the first priority of the government. ( )
3. Apartments were designed to allow married children to remain at home. ( )
4. When they were first built, danchi were for low income earners. ( )
5. Open plan apartments are more suitable for young people today. ( )

2 Write an answer to each question below.

1. What were two factors that affected housing availability after the war?

   _____

2. What modern facilities could be found in *danchi* apartments?

   _____

3. How were places for apartments in *danchi* allocated?

   _____

4. Why are companies changing the apartments to open plan style?

   _____

WRITING SECTION

WRITING FOCUS: Supporting Sentences

> **Supporting sentences** support the main idea stated in the topic sentence of a paragraph. We learned about topic sentences in Unit One and Two. Supporting sentences show why the topic sentence is true. Supporting sentences provide details using explanations, examples, statistics, or experts' opinions. Using them makes your opinion clearer and more believable. It is essential that supporting sentences clearly relate to both the topic and the focus of the topic. Let us look at a good and bad examples of supporting sentences.
>
> **Topic**: Tokyo
> **Focus of the topic**: *Places for shopping*
> **Topic sentence**: Tokyo has many *places for shopping*.
>
> ○ **Good example (a)**: The Ginza district in Tokyo has many fashionable stores, where shoppers can buy high quality goods.
>
> × **Bad example (b)**: Tokyo has two professional baseball stadiums, Meiji Jingu and Tokyo Dome.
>
> Supporting sentence (a) is related to the topic and focus of the topic. It is an example of a place to shop in Tokyo, so it works as a supporting sentence. Sentence (b) is related to the topic of the topic sentence. However, it does *not* follow the focus of the topic sentence. Therefore, it is unrelated to the overall topic sentence, and it does not work as a supporting sentence.

EXERCISE

1 Read paragraph 2 of the passage *Danchi: Changing Lifestyles*, **underline the supporting sentences** of the topic sentences, and **identify the type of support** (example, explanation, statistics, expert's opinion).

2 Read the model paragraph and answer the questions.

A MODEL PARAGRAPH

A Good Place to Live

The danchi where I grew up in the suburbs of Tokyo was a great place to live. It was a very comfortable place to live, with windows on both sides. It got a lot of southern sun and had a good flow of air. We didn't need to have an air conditioner. It was also a community-centered place to live. It was built with good access to public facilities, such as playgrounds and parks. I used to spend time after school in the park playing with my friends. There were shops on the ground floor of my building including a supermarket, dry cleaner, and a dentist. There was even a ramen shop where I often ate when my parents worked late. It was a wonderful place to live.
(128 words)

1. Underline the topic sentence of the paragraph.

2. The paragraph above gives two reasons why the place was a great place to live. What are they?

   _____   _____

3. For each reason, list three supporting details.

   For reason 1: _____ _____ _____

   For reason 2: _____ _____ _____

3 Write your paragraph (about 100 words) about a good place to live on a separate sheet of paper. Use the space below to plan. Write ideas, not full sentences.

WRITING

Topic: _____   **Focus:** A Good Place to Live

Reason 1:
   Support 1:
   Support 2:

Reason 2:
   Support 1:
   Support 2:

Reason 3:
   Support 1:
   Support 2:

Unit 4
Building Structure

READING SECTION

Sagrada Familia: Structure and Detail

　　Antonio Gaudi's Sagrada Familia in Barcelona is an architectural highlight of Spain. The church has been under construction since 1882 and is the most visited building in Spain. Even though it is a Catholic church, the Sagrada Familia invites all people to share
5 "love, harmony, good, generosity and peace."
　　The Sagrada Familia contains rich religious imagery and symbolism. Knowing the stories behind the imagery will help you understand the building better. For example, the name Sagrada Familia means Holy Family. It is the name given to the three-person family of Jesus, Mary and Joseph. Also, on each of the three facades of the building, visitors can see the story of different parts of the life of
10 Jesus in intricate detail. Religious imagery can also be seen in the structure of the cathedral. Each of the 18 spires in the church plans represents a different person in the Bible.
　　In building the Sagrada Familia, Gaudi was strongly influenced by nature. Even the height of the Sagrada Familia showed Gaudi's respect for nature. When it is completed, the Sagrada Familia will be the tallest church building in the world with the largest spire designed to be 172.5m. Gaudi
15 wanted to build an impressive building, but he believed the church should not be greater than God. Because of this, when he designed the building, he made sure its height was several meters lower than the nearby Montjuic, a hill overlooking Barcelona harbor.
　　Gaudi's plans for the Sagrada Familia were influenced by nature; however, he did not try to copy nature. He analyzed nature and used its principles when he designed the structure. An example of
20 this is Gaudi's observation of catenary. A catenary, which is commonly found in the physical world, is the curve formed when a rope or chain is hung between two fixed points. In Gaudi's case, he often made large chain and wire models of catenary in preference to using paper plans. The wire models showed a three dimensional image of the lines of the arches he planned to build in the cathedral. The catenary of the model were inverted in his mind and constructed as catenary arches inside the
25 Sagrada Familia.
　　Further inspiration from nature can also be seen in the effect of Gaudi's use of catenary arches in the interior of the Sagrada Familia. Arches branch out at a height giving the appearance of a vast white forest in the sky. The greater structural stability of the catenary arches means that Gaudi was able to retain the height and space of a Gothic cathedral without relying on the support of buttresses.
30 The Sagrada Familia is an extraordinarily original building. Both the interior and exterior are a testament to Gaudi's vision and technical skill and it seems fitting that he is buried inside the church. The Sagrada Familia is estimated to be completed by 2028. Its completion will finally realize Gaudi's dream.　(483 words)

Vocabulary

Sagrada Familia（サグラダファミリア）, under construction（建設中）, generosity（寛容）, religious imagery（宗教的なイメージ）, symbolism（象徴）, Holy Family（聖家族）, Jesus, Mary and Joseph（イエス, マリア, ヨセフ）, facade（ファサード, 正面）, intricate（複雑な）, cathedral（大聖堂）, spire（尖塔）, the Bible（聖書）, analyze（分析する）, principle（原理, 原則）, catenary（カテナリー曲線・カテナリーアーチ）, physical world（物質界, 物理的な世界）, fixed point（固定点, 不動点）, invert（逆になる）, inspiration（刺激・インスピレーション）, interior column（内柱）, branch out（〜から広がっている, 枝分かれする）, appearance（外見）, vast（広大な）, stability（安定感）, retain（〜を保っている）, rely on（〜に頼っている）, buttress（控え壁・バットレス）, extraordinarily（非常に）, testament（証明, 証）, fitting（ふさわしい, 適している）

Unit 4

Vocabulary Exercise

1 Find the closest meaning from a-e for each word below.

1. analyze ( )
2. vast ( )
3. facade ( )
4. intricate ( )
5. invert ( )

a. the front of a building
b. something complicated
c. consider in a detailed manner
d. turn upside down or inside out
e. something huge or enormous

2 Write the most appropriate word to complete the sentences. (You may need to change the form of the word.) There are some words in the box that you don't use.

1. The church, originally designed by Gaudi, has been (   ) for more than a century.
2. The catenary arches are not just beautiful, they also give the building greater (   ).
3. Gaudi's work was (   ) by religion and nature.
4. The Sagrada Familia has intricate pictures on its (   ).

| under construction | facade | inspiration | religious imagery | stability |

Comprehension Questions

1 Write T if the statement is true according to the text and F if it is not true.

1. The spires of the Sagrada Familia have a religious meaning. ( )
2. The Sagrada Familia is taller than Mont Monjuic. ( )
3. Gaudi preferred to use paper plans for designing the cathedral. ( )
4. Catenary arches give stability to the building. ( )
5. There are trees growing in the Sagrada Familia. ( )

2 Write an answer to each question below.

1. What can be found on the outside walls of the Sagrada Familia?

2. Why didn't Gaudi want the cathedral to be taller than the nearby hill?

3. How did Gaudi visualize catenary arches for the cathedral?

4. How is the image of a forest in the sky created?

WRITING SECTION

WRITING FOCUS: Cause and Effect Structures

What is a cause and effect structure?

A cause (C) is a reason that explains why some thing happens. e.g. It is hot. An effect (E) is what happens as a result of the cause. e.g. I took off my jacket. This relationship can be expressed in a variety of ways. Using expressions to show that something is a cause or an effect makes the relationship clear. Let's look at the following examples:

1. (C) The construction of the Sagrada Familia relied on private donations, (E) **so** progress in building it was slow.
2. (C) Gaudi respected nature. (E) **Therefore**, he did not want the Sagrada Familia to be taller than a nearby mountain.
3. (E) Many tourists visit the Sagrada Familia every year **because** (C) it is famous.
4. (C) **Since** architectural technology has advanced, (E) The Sagrada Familia may be completed by 2030.

Several transitional expressions

To Show *Causes*
- because [sentence]
- result from [noun phrase]
- when [sentence]
- because of [noun phrase]
- since [sentence]
- due to [noun phrase]

To Show *Effects*
- so [sentence]
- one effect/result is
- therefore/thus, [sentence]
- as a result, [sentence]
- consequently, [sentence]

Unit 4

EXERCISE

1 Read the model paragraph and follow the directions below.

A MODEL PARAGRAPH

The Failure of the Pruitt-Igoe Apartment Buildings

The Pruitt-Igoe apartment buildings of Saint Louis, Missouri were pulled down by the U.S. government in 1972 because they had become a place of serious crime. There are different explanations for the failure. Some people blame architectural features, such as elevators. To save money, the elevators were built so that they only stopped on every third floor. As a result, residents had to use dark stairways to get to their floor. Because of this, the stairways became a place for crimes such as robberies. Other people believe that social problems were to blame. When the economy declined and unemployment increased, living conditions in the housing projects declined. Since living conditions declined, the housing projects became a place of crime. This complex case will be studied for many more years. (129 words)

1. Circle the cause and effect transitional expressions used in the model paragraph.

2. Underline the CAUSE(S). Draw a wavy line under the EFFECT(S).

2 Choose the correct word(s) to complete sentences. Make sure to clearly express cause and effect relationship.

1. The buildings were pulled down (because / so) there was too much crime.
2. There was too much crime, (because / so) the buildings were pulled down.
3. The buildings were pulled down. (Therefore / Since) the residents needed to find somewhere else to live.
4. The residents needed to find somewhere else to live, (therefore / since) the buildings were pulled down.
5. The elevators didn't stop on every floor, (because of / resulting in) people needing to use the stairs.
6. (Since / So) the elevators didn't stop on every floor, people had to use the stairs.
7. (Due to / Since) the poor economic situation, the living conditions were bad.

3 Write two sentences about your neighborhood using cause and effect structures.

(the public library) *The public library* is very quiet, **so** I often go there to study on the weekends.

(100 yen shop)

_____

(convenience store)

_____

Unit 5
Kitchen

READING SECTION

The Development of Kitchens and Lifestyle

In the development of modern living environments, kitchens have undergone significant changes. These changes reflect technological and social developments through time. In the Roman Empire, ordinary people cooked in public kitchens because they did not have them in their own homes. Once open fires were integrated into homes, kitchens began to take on new functions for the home and the family.

In Europe during the Middle Ages, it was common for people to cook food on an open fire in the center of one-room houses, similar to traditional Japanese *irori*. The open fire was also a source of heat and light. However, these one-room "farmhouse kitchens" had serious design flaws. Farmhouse kitchens produced great amounts of smoke and ash, which made staying in them for a long period of time uncomfortable. The invention of the chimney improved the situation dramatically; it allowed smoke and ash to escape the room entirely. With the invention of the chimney, the fire moved from the middle of the room to a fireplace against the wall. The new position of the fire facilitated the development of a small kitchen area. For example, the Wyckoff House, the oldest remaining house of European colonizers in Brooklyn, New York, has a small kitchen area equipped with a chimney, large pots, and long metal roasting poles. These new kitchen areas were the basis of the modern kitchen.

These days homes commonly have full kitchens with gas or electric ovens instead of simple kitchen areas with chimneys. Other kitchen appliances, such as refrigerators, dishwashers, and microwaves, have added further convenience to kitchens. Many of these appliances helped reduce the time that needs to be spent in food preparation. For example, once a household has a refrigerator, it is no longer necessary to spend time doing food shopping every day. A household with a rice-cooker can put the rice on to cook overnight and have it ready to eat when the household wakes up.

At the same time as appliances have enabled households to save time, kitchen design has helped make cooking a more social activity. There is a trend in house design to integrate the kitchen into the living space of the house. For example, some open kitchens have bar counters, where visitors can sit and interact with the host while he prepares the meal. Kitchen users now no longer need to be separated from others while doing kitchen work. This has led to kitchens becoming a hub of socializing during parties and other in-home social gatherings.

In a sense, kitchens have now come full circle since once again they are often the center of life in a home. The evolution of kitchens shows that their design impacts our lifestyle. This fact invites us to wonder how new kitchen innovations will affect lifestyles in the future. (466 words)

Vocabulary

undergo（経験する、受ける）, reflect（反映する）, the Roman Empire（ローマ帝国）, ordinary（普通の）, integrate（組み込む、統合する）, the Middle Ages（中世）, common（一般的）, source of heat（熱源）, flaw（弱点）, invention（発明）, chimney（煙突）, dramatically（劇的に）, entirely（完全に）, facilitate（容易にする、促進する）, the Wyckoff Farmhouse（ウィッコフ農家）, remaining（残っている）, colonizer（入植者、開拓者）, equipped（設備が整った）, roasting pole（ロースト棒）, appliance（電化製品）, refrigerator（冷蔵庫）, dishwasher（食洗機）, microwave（電子レンジ）, further（さらなる）, convenience（利便性）, reduce（削減する）, trend（傾向、流行）, interact（会話をする）, no longer（もはや〜ではない）, hub（中心、拠点）, gathering（集まり）, in a sense（ある意味）, come full circle（もとに戻る）, evolution（進化）, invite（〜させる、いざなう）, wonder（…かと思う）, innovation（革新）

Vocabulary Exercise

1 Find the closest meaning from a-e for each word below.

1. undergo ( )
2. flaw ( )
3. integrate ( )
4. facilitate ( )
5. gathering ( )

a. weakness, defect
b. combine two or more things, unify
c. meeting
d. experience
e. make something possible or easier

2 Write the most appropriate word to complete the sentences. (You may need to change the form of the word). There are some words in the box that you don't use.

1. We painted the wall by ourselves to (   ) the cost.
2. Electricity is one of the (   ) sources of energy in Japan.
3. Many old wooden houses still (   ) in the village.
4. This kitchen is well (   ) with state-of-the-art appliances.

| remain | convenience | reduce | common | equip | interact |

Comprehension Questions

1 Write T if the statement is true according to the text and F if it is not true.

1. Families in Roman times often shared kitchens with others. ( )
2. *Irori* originally came from Europe. ( )
3. Cooking facilities on the side walls helped to reduce the size of space for cooking. ( )
4. Chimneys are regaining popularity. ( )
5. Kitchens remain at the center of the home. ( )

2 Write an answer to each question below.

1. What problems did fires inside the home have?

   _____

2. What improved the problems caused by fires inside the home?

   _____

3. What has been a benefit of appliances in the kitchen?

   _____

4. How does a refrigerator save time for a household?

   _____

WRITING SECTION

WRITING FOCUS: Giving Examples

One effective way to support your topic sentence is by giving clear examples in the supporting sentences. By using the following expressions, you can make sure that the readers understand that you are giving examples. The following list of expressions can be used to signal that an example will follow:
- For example, [a sentence.]
- For instance, [a sentence.]
- To illustrate, [a sentence.]
- To give an example, [a sentence.]

When these expressions are used at the beginning of the sentence, it is very important to make sure that it is followed by a sentence.

Example 1:
The style of Japanese and western kitchens are quite different. **For instance**, it is not common for Japanese kitchens to have a built-in oven.

Example 2:
There are some similarities between Middle Age kitchens in Japan and Europe. **To give an example**, the European farmhouse kitchen is similar to the Japanese *irori* kitchen.

The following expressions can be used in the middle of a sentence signal that you are going to give an example.

> for example   for instance   such as   like   ...., e.g., ...

Example 3:
There are various kitchen styles, **e.g.,** one-wall kitchens, L-shaped kitchens, and island kitchens.

Example 4:
Kitchen appliances, **like** refrigerators and dishwashers, are constantly evolving.

EXERCISE

1 Find the mistakes in the following example sentences. Then, rewrite them in a way that is correct. There may be more than one way to correct each sentence.

1. Chimneys led to the creation of small kitchen areas. Such as the Wyckoff House has a small kitchen area with a chimney, large pots, and long metal roasting poles.

   _____.

2. These days, many kitchens have modern appliances. For example microwaves and refrigerators are widely used.

   _____.

3. There is a trend among designers to integrate kitchens into the living space, to illustrate, some open kitchens have bar counters.

   _____

4. "Farmhouse kitchens" had serious design flaws. Like they produced great amounts of smoke and ash.

   _____

2 Read the model paragraph and follow the directions below.

A MODEL PARAGRAPH

Inspiration from Nature

Many pieces of architecture have been inspired by nature. Architects may use the form, color, and characteristics of nature to guide their designs. For example, the Beijing National Stadium looks like an extraordinary metallic bird's nest, and the circular rooftop symbolizes the sky. By using this design, architects hoped to show the coexistence of nature and the Olympic Games. Other architectural designs, such as the Taipei 101 building, are also inspired by nature. The Taipei 101 building in particular looks like a large bamboo plant, a symbol of strength and growth. The building is a shade of bamboo green and is divided into sections that look like bamboo joints. Architects will surely continue to be inspired by nature when designing human-made structures. (122 words)

1. Circle the expressions that signal examples used in the model paragraph.

2. The main idea of the model paragraph is that architecture is inspired by nature. List the two examples that support this idea. For each example, list the natural elements that provide the inspiration.

   example 1: _____   Natural element(s): _____
   example 2: _____   Natural element(s): _____

3. Read the example sentence below. Choose your own buildings. Write your own sentences giving the source of inspiration and the example(s). Use the expressions you have learned.

   e.g. The Sagrada Familia was inspired by nature. For example, the interior looks like a giant, white forest in the sky.

   a) _____

   _____

   b) _____

   _____

GROUND FLOOR   FIRST FLOOR

Unit 6
Living Room

READING SECTION

An Architect's Own House 7

Architects express their ideas through their work. The best expression of their ideas can often be found in the way they design their own houses. Let's look at the Red House, a red brick neo-Gothic building in the
5 suburbs of London. The Red House was designed by the English designer William Morris in 1859. He designed it with the help of his architect friend Philip Webb. Morris and his wife, Jane, are remembered today for being founders of the Arts and Craft Movement. The Red House remains a monument to their ideas of art, craftsmanship, and lifestyle more than 150 years after it was built.

The design of the Red House was different from the homes typically built by gentry of the
10 era. At that time, many buildings were built in a Georgian style, which was influenced by classical ideas including symmetry in design. In contrast, the Red House looked to Gothic architecture for inspiration. In designing the Red House, Morris did not want to be constrained by classical symmetry and wanted the house to be convenient and user-friendly for the inhabitants. For example, rather than being forced to have windows that looked balanced on the outside, windows in the Red
15 House were located according to the needs of each room.

The Red House reflected Morris' belief that attractive surroundings were necessary for producing good work. The Arts and Crafts Movement placed a high value on craftsmanship and manual labor. It rejected the mass-produced goods that had become common through the Industrial Revolution. Morris was critical of the cheap, poor-quality, factory-made products that were flooding the market,
20 believing they had a negative effect on both the craftspeople and consumers. He thought that everything in a home should be useful or beautiful. In the Red House, Morris' commitment to the work of craftspeople can be seen in features such as tapestries, stained glass, and built-in furniture.

The layout of the Red House gives us an insight into the society of the age in which it was built. The home provided space for both living and entertaining. On the second floor, above the dining
25 room, is the "drawing room." In upper-middle-class homes, gentlemen enjoyed after-dinner political discussion with alcohol in the dining room. Ladies who didn't care for the political chat "withdrew" to the drawing room on the upper floor to relax. The word drawing room comes from the word -*withdraw* - which means "leave a place." The word drawing room is still sometimes used to indicate a formal room for entertaining guests; however, these days both men and women share the space.
30 The Red House has become a museum and remains as a reminder of the era and Morris' philosophy. If you have a chance to visit London, why don't you enjoy the firsthand experience of Morris' house? (468 words)   (Based on the Japanese passage written by Prof. Yoko Ito of Shibaura Institute of Technology)

Vocabulary

design（デザインする）, brick（レンガ）, neo-Gothic（ネオゴシック）, suburb（郊外）, founder（設立者）, craftsmanship（職人の技能）, typically（典型的に、概して）, Georgian style（ジョージ様式）, influence（影響を受ける）, symmetry（（左右）対称、調和）, in contrast（一方）, Gothic（ゴシック様式の）, inspiration（インスピレーション）, constrain（無理やりさせる、制約する）, inhabitant（住民）, look balanced（バランス良く見える）, attractive surrounding（魅力的な環境、周囲）, place a high value（高い価値を置く）, manual labor（肉体労働）, reject（反対する）, mass-produced goods（大量製品、大量産物）, Industrial Revolution（産業革命）, critical（批判的）, factory-made product（工場製品）, flood（〜であふれている）, commitment（約束、責任）, feature（特徴）, tapestry（タペストリー）, stained glass（ステンドグラス）, built-in furniture（備え付けの家具）, insight（識見）, entertaining（喜ぶ、（客に）おもてなしをする）, drawing room（客間、応接間、ドローイングルーム）, upper-middle-class（上位中産階級）, withdraw（退散する、引き上げる）, indicate（示す）, firsthand（直接に）

Unit 6

Vocabulary Exercise

1 Find the closest meaning from a-e for each word below.

1. founder ( )
2. inhabitant ( )
3. constrain ( )
4. feature ( )
5. firsthand ( )

a. directly
b. a characteristic or special aspect of something
c. control or limit something
d. a person who lives in a place
e. a person who establishes an institution

2 Write the most appropriate word to complete the sentences. (You may need to change the form of the word.) There are some words in the box that you don't use.

1. In 1859, William Morris (   ) the Red House.
2. The design of the Red House differed from (   ) homes of the era.
3. The Red House was designed for (   ) to live comfortably.
4. There is a space for living and (   ) in the Red House.

| design | reject | typically | tapestry | inhabitant | entertaining |

COMPREHENSION QUESTIONS

1 Write T if the statement is true according to the text and F if it is not true.

1. Philip Webb founded the Arts and Crafts Movement ( )
2. Symmetry provides freedom in design. ( )
3. The Red House was inspired by neo-Gothic buildings. ( )
4. Morris believed that aesthetics were important in a work environment. ( )
5. A drawing room was used mainly for art. ( )

2 Write an answer to each question below.

1. What was the common style of building at the time the Red House was built?

   _____

2. What did the Art and Crafts Movement believe was important?

   _____

3. What can be seen in the house that shows appreciation of manual labor?

   _____

4. What is different about drawing rooms in the past and drawing rooms today?

   _____

WRITING SECTION

WRITING FOCUS: Compare and Contrast Structures

What are comparison and contrast sentences?

In our everyday life, we often make decisions. To make a decision, it is important to compare and contrast options. When we compare, we find and explain **similarities** between things or ideas. When we contrast, we find and explain **differences** between things or ideas. Comparing and contrasting is a basic part of life. For example, before taking a class, you compare and contrast the features of each class you might take.

Comparison and contrast structures are important when writing a paper. When we compare and contrast at least two things or ideas, we often try to persuade the reader that our view is correct. Therefore, comparison and contrast structures are important for writing persuasively.

When you find similarities for two or more things or ideas, **comparison** structures are useful. When you find differences for two or more things or ideas, **contrast** structures are useful.

The following expressions are useful for showing similarity (or comparison) and difference (or contrast).

Basic structures of comparison

| Both A and B ... | Not only A but also B ... | A as well as B ... | Neither A nor B ... |
| In addition to A, B ... | In the same way ... | Similarly, ... | Likewise, ... |

Basic structures of contrast

A···., but/yet B ...   A .... On the other hand/While/However, B ...
A ···.. In contrast, B ...   Compared to/with A, B is ...

Basic structures for contrasting different features of the same thing

Although A ..., A ...   Though A ..., A ...

EXERCISE

1 Read the model paragraph and follow the directions below.

A MODEL PARAGRAPH

2D Drawings and 3D Computer Models

   Both drawings and computer models are important media for architects. Drawings are used for two-dimensional representation of architectural design. In contrast, computer models are used for mostly three-dimensional study and presentation. Conventional drawings are a commonly accepted communication medium for architects, engineers, contractors, and clients. On the other hand, computer models are used for three-dimensional volume study or rendering, and also for coordination or simulation. When architects need to discuss floor plans, two-dimensional drawings are more suitable. However, if they want to show perspectives from multiple angles, a computer model works better. Today, we have many choices of media available. It is very important for architects to use the most appropriate media for their purpose. (115 words)

1. What are the two things that are being compared and contrasted in the paragraph?

   _____ and _____

2. Circle the expressions that signal comparison and contrast used in the model paragraph.

3. Identify each comparison and contrast in the model paragraph. For each one, circle "comparison" or "contrast" and write it on the lines below.
   (comparison/contrast): _____
   (comparison/contrast): _____
   (comparison/contrast): _____
   (comparison/contrast): _____

2 Write a "comparison and contrast" paragraph on a separate sheet of paper. Follow the steps.

1. Pick two items to compare and contrast.

   _____ and _____

2. Find and list similarities and differences between items.
   (similarity/difference): _____
   (similarity/difference): _____
   (similarity/difference): _____

3. Change the list into complete sentences. Here, try to use lots of expressions from the opening part of the writing section.

   _____
   _____
   _____

4. Choose the most important similarities and differences which you listed.

5. Think of a main idea which includes an overall view of the similarities and differences.

   _____

6. Based on your main idea, write a topic sentence.

   _____

7. Keep the most important comparison and contrast sentences you made as supporting sentences.

Unit 7
Design Styles

READING SECTION

Architecture and Comfort

Science and technology have a mission to enrich people's lives. As a part of science and technology, architecture shares the same goal. One of the ways that architects accomplish this goal is by creating comfort. Before architects try to make a comfortable environment, an important question for them to consider is, "What does 'comfortable' really mean?"

Environmental elements help us explain comfort. Wherever you are, you feel light, sound, heat, and air with your five senses (hearing, seeing, tasting, touching, and smelling). What your five senses perceive, such as temperature, the degree of light, and the loudness of a room, are environmental elements. We perceive through our sense organs, namely, our eyes, ears, nose, tongue, and skin. When our sense organs receive a pleasant physical stimulation in an environment, that environment is a comfort.

Many things affect environmental elements, which ultimately determine whether we receive a pleasant physical stimulation (comfort) or not. The structure, materials, thickness, and color of walls affect environmental elements. For example, on a cold day, sitting on a metal chair makes you feel cold, while sitting on a cushioned wooden chair makes you feel warm. The heat of the chair itself is an environmental element. When the chair comes into contact with our skin (a sense organ), a signal is sent to our brain, which tells us that the temperature is cold or warm. If this sensation is pleasant, then the chair you sit in is a comfort. Likewise, the height of ceilings, the location and the size of windows also affect environmental elements. A big window can bring in a lot of sunshine and make the room brighter, while a small window will only allow a small bit of sunlight into the room. The brightness of the room itself is an environmental element. When the light enters our eyes (another sense organ), a different signal is sent to our brain, which tells us that the light is bright or dim. Again, if the sensation is pleasant, then the room is a comfort.

Architects can create comfort by controlling the effects of environmental elements. How they do so differs depending on surrounding conditions. On a hot tropical island, houses which let the breeze go through make the room feel cooler and pleasant. In other words, the open design of such a house in these surroundings leads to more comfort. On the other hand, in a place with a harsh winter, creating thick walls that preserve warmth leads to more comfort.

In the field of architectural environment studies, we study how the conditions of light, sound, heat, air, and others can create comfort. We also study how spaces should be designed. We focus on how we can create comfortable spaces for people. This helps us reach the goal of architecture: enriching people's lives. (466 words)

(Based on the Japanese passage written by Dr. Hiroshi Furuya of Shibaura Institute of Technology)

Vocabulary

mission (使命), enrich (豊かにする), accomplish (達成する), comfort (居心地), comfortable (心地よい), consider (配慮する), five senses (五感), perceive (感知する), sense organ (感覚器官), tongue (舌), pleasant (快適(な)), physical stimulation (物理的刺激), ultimately (究極的に), determine (決定する), sensation (感覚), likewise (同様に), ceiling (天井), dim (薄暗い), differ (異なる), harsh (厳しい), preserve (保つ), warmth (暖かさ)

Unit 7

Vocabulary Exercise

1 Find the closest meaning from a-e for each word below.

1. enrich ( )
2. determine ( )
3. ultimately ( )
4. dim ( )
5. harsh ( )

a. to decide
b. not having much light
c. severe
d. to improve the quality
e. in the end

2 Write the most appropriate word to complete the sentences. (You may need to change the form of the word.) There are some words in the box that you don't use.

1. The relaxing color of the wall makes the room ( ).
2. Normally the ( ) of a room is a light color.
3. Having a heater in the room provides ( ).
4. Our hard work helped us to ( ) our goal.

| warmth | preserve | pleasant | accomplish | ceiling | tongue |

Comprehension Questions

1 Write T if the statement is true according to the text and F if it is not true.

1. Architects enrich the senses. ( )
2. Perception is more important than environmental elements. ( )
3. The five senses are important for perceiving comfort. ( )
4. Metal chairs are warmer than cushioned chairs. ( )
5. Thick walls are suitable in places that have typhoons. ( )

2 Write an answer to each question below.

1. What do architecture and science and technology have in common?

   _____

2. What enables us to recognize environmental elements?

   _____

3. What are pleasant sensations perceived as?

   _____

4. How can the design of a building be adapted for a tropical climate?

   _____

WRITING SECTION

WRITING FOCUS: What is a Persuasive Essay? — Organization of a Persuasive Essay and Brainstorming for a Thesis Statement

Persuasive essays try to make readers believe the opinion is true. This is done by giving reasons to support your opinion. Examples of topic sentences of persuasive essays are
"Tokyo is a good place for international students to study,"
"Wooden houses are better than concrete houses," and
"Every town should have a big park."

In the **introduction**, state your main opinion. You want your readers to believe your opinion. Your main opinion is called the **thesis statement**. Like a topic sentence, a thesis statement should have a topic and a topic focus and should not be too broad. The next paragraphs are called **body paragraphs**. Each body paragraph gives one reason for believing that the thesis statement (your main opinion) is true. In general, you should have at least three reasons (body paragraphs) to make the thesis statement believable. Lastly, in the **conclusion**, paraphrase your thesis statement and summarize your supporting sentences to bring the essay to a smooth ending.

Organization of a persuasive essay

Introduction	State your opinion
Body	Reason 1
	Reason 2
	Reason 3
Conclusion	Summary

How to find a topic that you want to write about

Brainstorming is a useful way to find a thesis statement. To brainstorm, simply write down as many ideas as you can. As soon as you think of an idea, write it down. A brainstorm is a list of ideas which can later be organized or used to select an idea for your essay. To brainstorm for a thesis statement, write as many opinions down as possible which you might want to convince your readers about.

(a) Topic idea examples:
- The best place to ....
- A feature all buildings should have
- The most inspirational ....
- All architects should ...

(b) Useful language for a persuasive essay:
- _____ is/are better than _____.
- _____ is/are the best _____.
- Every _____ should have a _____.
- Everyone should _____ (at least once, everyday, etc.)
- _____ is the best way to/ place to/ kind of _____.
- In the future _____ will (be) _____.

EXERCISE

1 Look at thesis statements below then brainstorm and write your own ideas.

A MODEL BRAINSTORM

Brainstorming for Thesis Statement

o Japanese traditional houses are better than Western houses.
o Every home should have a solar panel.
o The Sagrada Familia is the best architecture in the world.
o In the future, all energy will be renewable.
o ... ...
o ... ...

Possible thesis statements
- _____
- _____
- _____
- _____

2 **Peer feedback**

1. Get into pairs. Tell your partner your thesis statements. Explain why they are good. After you discuss them, give feedback to your partner by answering the following questions.
    - Which thesis statements do you think are the best?
    - Why do you think they are the best?
    - How could they be improved?
    - Does each thesis statement have a clear topic and topic focus?

2. First, consider the feedback you received to improve the thesis statements. Then choose which thesis statement you like the most. This will be the thesis statement of your essay. You will use this statement in the remaining chapters of this book.

Thesis statement: _____

Unit 8
Scales and Dimensions

READING SECTION

Le Corbusier's Modulor

Most people know that Le Corbusier was influential in modern architecture. His importance can be seen in the decision in 2016 to award World Heritage status to a body of his work across seven countries. The "Five Points of New Architecture" developed by Le Corbusier have become part of mainstream architecture and bring greater freedom to building design. Another development of Le Corbusier worth mentioning is his original system of measurement called Modulor.

In Le Corbusier's era, France had already been using the metric system for almost a century. The metric system is easy to calculate; however, it is derived from the meridians of the globe, and unlike the imperial system of feet and inches, has no connection to the human body. Le Corbusier believed that human proportions should be integral to architecture. He wanted to integrate human proportions into the metric system. To achieve this, he devised Modulor.

Modulor drew on Vitruvius' ideals of proportions, which can be seen in Da Vinci's Vitruvian man. Vitruvius understood the ideal male human body in terms of ratios, e.g., the height of a man was equal to the width of his outstretched arms, and the size of the palm was equal to the width of four fingers. Le Corbusier's system of proportions was also influenced by the aesthetically pleasing Golden Ratio, which had been studied since the time of Euclid. Le Corbusier, like Vitruvius and Euclid, believed that mathematical proportions based on the human body gave beauty, harmony and balance to structures.

In addition to aesthetically pleasing mathematical proportions, Modulor also had a numerical scale. This was graphically represented by "Modulor Man." Modulor Man had an actual height: 6 feet or 1.83 m. This was Le Corbusier's height for an ideal man. Modulor was a way to create a standardized scale that bridged the gap between the metric and imperial systems. This scale became integral to his structures and standardized the sizes of his building elements, for example, the height and width of doors and windows, wall panels, windows and pavers. The regulated spacing of these elements gives harmony and rhythm to le Corbusier's buildings.

Le Corbusier translated his Modulor theory into practice in a number of his works; the most famous of these is Unité d'habitation in Marseilles. Le Corbusier also had the opportunity to use Modulor on a large scale in the early 1950s when he became involved with the creation of a planned city, Chandigarh, in the newly-independent India. He believed that using a human scale for the city could create an environment where people could live a full and harmonious life. He saw the city as a model of hope for a better future. Although the success of the project is still debated, there is no doubt that infusing human scale was an attempt to improve the quality of architecture. With the invention of Modulor, Le Corbusier was able to retain the simplicity of the metric system while standardizing the sizes of building elements based on a human scale.   (500 words)

(Based on the Japanese passage written by Dr. Fumitoshi Kumazawa of Shibaura Institute of Technology)

Vocabulary

influential（影響力のある）, body of his work（一連の作品）, "Five Points of New Architecture"（「新しい建築の５つの要点」）, mainstream（主流）, "Modulor"（モジュロール）, metric system（メートル法）, meridians of the globe（地球の子午線）, imperial system（ヤード・ポンド法）, integral（不可欠な）, Vitruvius（ウィトルウィウス：共和政ローマ期に活動した建築家）, proportion（割合）, integrate（統合する）, Vitruvian man（ウィトルウィウス的人体図）, ratio（比（率））, outstretched（広げた）, aesthetically pleasing（美的な喜び）, Golden Ratio（黄金比）, Euclid（ユークリッド原論）, scale（目盛り）, graphically（視覚的に）, ideal man（理想的な人体）, standardized（基準の、一般化された）, paver（舗装版、ペーバー）, regulated spacing（基準の間隔）

Unit 8

Vocabulary Exercise

1 Find the closest meaning from a-d for each word below.

1. mainstream ( )
2. ideal ( )
3. standardized ( )
4. integral ( )
5. ratio ( )

a. a way of comparing quantities
b. a necessary part of
c. to make things of a similar type the same
d. the best or most suitable / perfect
e. accepted as being usual / commonly thought

2 Write the most appropriate word to complete the sentences. (You may need to change the form of the word.) There are some words in the box that you don't use.

1. Le Corbusier believed architecture should be based on human needs, so when he developed Modulor, human (   ) were an important component.
2. Le Corbusier has (   ) modern architecture; ideas he introduced have become widely accepted.
3. The (   ) system uses non-metric units, such as feet and inches.
4. The Golden Ratio is said to give balance and harmony and make artwork (   ) pleasing.

| scale | influence | imperial | proportion | derive | aesthetically |

Comprehension Questions

1 Write T if the statement is true according to the text and F if it is not true.

1. The World Heritage Award for Le Corbusier's work was given for buildings in multiple countries. ( )
2. Le Corbusier believed the metric system improved architecture. ( )
3. The Modulor Man was based on Da Vinci's height. ( )
4. Many of Le Corbusier's buildings have a standerdized scale. ( )
5. Modulor was designed to simplify people's lives. ( )

2 Write an answer to each question below.

1. How is the metric system derived?

   _____

2. What is the advantage of the metric system?

   _____

3. For Le Corbusier, what was the advantage of the imperial system?

   _____

4. What did Le Corbusier combine with the idea of human proportions to create Modulor?

   _____

WRITING SECTION

WRITING FOCUS: Creating the Outline of Your Essay

Now that you have brainstormed a thesis statement for your essay, it is time to think of reasons which support your opinion. This can also be done by brainstorming. Brainstorming for supporting ideas can be done by turning your thesis statement into a question, and we call the question a "thesis question." Let us consider the following thesis statement:

Thesis statement: Every town should have a big park.
This thesis statement can be turned into the following thesis question:

Thesis Question: Why should every town have a big park?
Answers to the thesis question support the thesis statement.
- Children can play there safely.
- It is a place for people in the community to gather.
- It improves the landscape of the town.
- It is a place for animals to live.
- People can exercise in the park.
- It improves the air quality of the town.
- ... ...

These sentences are now reasons for why the thesis statement is true. In other words, they are the reasons which support the thesis statement.

EXERCISE

1 Brainstorming for Reasons

1. Write the thesis statement you have chosen on the top line of the "Brainstorming for Reasons" box below.

2. Turn your thesis statement into a question on the next line.

3. Brainstorm by writing as many answers to the thesis question as you can next to the dots.

```
Brainstorming for Reasons

Thesis statement: _____

Thesis question: _____

Reasons:
    • _____
    • _____
    • _____
```

4. Revise the reasons you wrote so that they are full sentences.

5. Get into pairs. Explain to your partner why the reasons you wrote down are good ones. After you discuss them, give feedback to your partner by answering the following questions.
   - Which reasons do you think are the best for answering the thesis question?
   - Why do you think they are the best?
   - How could they be improved?
   - Does each thesis statement have a clear topic and topic focus?

6. Choose the reasons that you think are the best. After you have finished, the reasons you wrote will be the topic sentences of your body paragraphs.

2 Make your own outline

Using the example outline below, make your own outline. In the "Introduction" box, write your thesis statement. In the "Body" boxes, write your topic sentences in the order you will introduce them in your essay. Do not worry about the "conclusion" box. We will learn more about this part of the essay later.

Model outline

Introduction	Every town should have a big park.
Body	It improves the air quality of the town.
	People can exercise in the park.
	It is a place for people in the community to gather.
Conclusion	Summary and comment

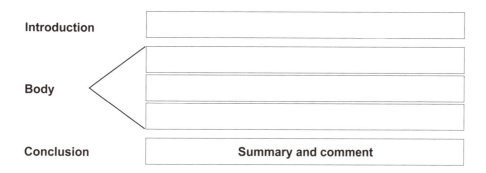

Introduction	
Body	
Conclusion	Summary and comment

Unit 9
Colors

READING SECTION

Colors: Culture and the International Visual Language

In architecture, color is one of the most important aspects of decoration; however, color has a much deeper significance as well. The relationship between color and humans has cultural, psychological, and physiological aspects. These features are like a window to see into the hearts and minds of people. Once the window is opened, it can be used by architects to create spaces which meet various needs of people.

Color has expressed cultural meanings throughout history and into the present. For ancient Greeks, color represented high status. Gold and other vibrant colors were used to paint temples to express the superiority of the gods. Color continues to contain cultural meanings, for instance, representing gender. In America, since the 1950s, blue, which was formerly seen as a girl's color, has come to represent boys, while pink has come to represent girls. Boys' rooms are often painted blue, whereas girls' rooms are often pink. In addition to its cultural representations, color can also have psychological effects on people.

Study of the psychological effects of color originated with the American Faber Birren, the so-called "father of color psychology." Birren, who established the profession of "color consultant" in 1936, believed that the study of color is a mental and psychological science. The influence of color on the psychology of humans can be seen in the way perceptions of time can be altered by the use of color. One study found that exposure to warm colors, such as red, orange, or yellow, make people feel that they have spent a longer amount of time in a room, while exposure to cool colors, such as blue, green, and purple, makes people feel that they have spent less time in a room. Architects can use this knowledge to their advantage. For example, warm colors suit restaurant interiors because they make people feel that they have spent a long time eating, drinking, and talking. As a result, customers are likely to leave earlier. This leaves space for new customers to come. In contrast, painting a meeting room with warm colors might make employees feel that they have been in meetings for too long. The psychological effect of color can be so strong that it can affect people physiologically.

Studies on the impact of color have found that they can affect people physiologically. For example, the perception of red has been shown to make people feel excited and stimulated, and as a result, can raise their blood pressure. Blue has the opposite effect; people who perceive blue feel calmer and more relaxed. Remarkably, similar effects have been observed in blindfolded people due to the effects that red and blue light waves have on the body. Since these reactions are not specific to a particular culture, some researchers believe that color is an "international visual language."

Learning about color enables architects to create spaces that suit the needs of their clients. Architects who spend time understanding the international language of color can create environments that are not just aesthetically pleasing but also improve people's well-being. (504 words)

Vocabulary

psychological（心理的な）, feature（特色, 主要点）, ancient Greeks（古代ギリシャ）, high status（重要な地位）, vibrant（鮮やかな）, superiority（優位）, gender（性別）, formerly（以前は）, whereas（一方）, originated（由来される）, establish（創案する）, mental（精神的な）, perception（知覚, 認知）, alter（変化する）, exposure to（さらされる）, suit（適している）, in contrast（対照的に）, employee（被雇用者, 従業員）, impact（印象）, stimulated（刺激を受ける）, remarkably（著しく）, specific（特別の）

Vocabulary Exercise

1 Find the closest meaning from a-e for each word below.

1. vibrant (　)
2. perception (　)
3. alter (　)
4. specific (　)
5. superiority (　)

a. being more important, stronger, or better
b. particular
c. change, modify
d. vivid
e. the way people understand or feel about something

2 Write the most appropriate word to complete the sentences. (You may need to change the form of the word.) There are some words in the box that you don't use.

1. Cool colors may not (　　　　) places where you want to create a cozy feeling.
2. The company owner asked his (　　　　) about their working conditions.
3. The colorful design is the (　　　　) of this architect in many of his works.
4. They discovered ancient wall paintings that still had (　　　　) colors.

| stimulated | feature | vibrant | atmosphere | employee | suit |

Comprehension Questions

1 Write T if the statement is true according to the text and F if it is not true.

1. The ancient Greeks painted gods to show respect. (　)
2. Blue used to be seen as a girls' color. (　)
3. Blue is considered to be a calming color. (　)
4. Color affects our sense of time. (　)
5. Warm colors are recommended for meeting rooms. (　)

2 Write an answer to each question below.

1. What was used to show the status of the ancient Greek gods?

   _____

2. What is an example of a color changing meaning?

   _____

3. How did Faber Birren describe the study of color?

   _____

4. Why are colors like red and yellow suitable for restaurants?

   _____

WRITING SECTION

WRITING FOCUS: Introduction

With a simple outline of your essay completed, it is time to write the introductory paragraph. An introduction often has an **attention getter** (also called a hook), which is a sentence that makes the audience interested in the topic. This is the first sentence of the introduction. When writing an attention getter, try to think of a reason why people would want to read about your topic. The thesis statement should be placed directly after the attention getter. After the thesis statement, you should introduce the reasons which support your opinion. These are simply the topic sentences of your body paragraphs. The final sentence of the introduction should smoothly transition into the next paragraph. This is called a **concluding sentence**.

The Structure of an Introduction

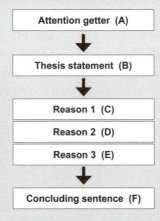

A MODEL INTRODUCTORY PARAGRAPH

(A) As we hurry from one place to the next in modern cities and towns, it is easy for us to forget about the benefits of nature and open spaces that parks provide. (B) However, every town should have a big park. (C) First, parks improve the air quality of the towns and cities that they are in. (D) Second, people can exercise in parks. (E) Third, parks are places where people in the community can gather. (F) Each of these benefits is essential for making our urban environments more livable. (91 words)

EXERCISE

1 Attention Getter

Write a few possible attention getters for your introduction. One way to make an attention getter is to give a context for your thesis statement. For example, suppose that your thesis statement is the following:

Every town in Japan should have a big park.

You may want to give a context for your discussion by adding the following attention getter:

Compared to European and American towns and cities, parks in Japan are rare.

You may need a transition word to connect the two sentences so that the attention getter flows into the thesis statement, as in the following:

Compared to European and American towns and cities, parks in Japan are rare. However, every town in Japan should have a big park.

Now, try to write your own attention getter.

2 Concluding Sentence of an Introductory Paragraph

Write a few possible concluding sentences for your introduction. One way to make a concluding sentence in an introductory paragraph is to emphasize the importance of the topic. Suppose again that your thesis statement is "Every town in Japan should have a big park." You might then write one of the following concluding sentences in your introduction:

- *As we will see, the health of Japanese communities in part depends on the number of parks they have.*
- *It is important that city planners as well as citizens keep the benefits of parks in mind for future generations.*

Now, try to write your own concluding sentence of an introductory paragraph.

3 Write the Introduction of Your Essay

Write your own introduction on a separate sheet of paper. Keep the structure of introductions in mind when you are writing. You may want to use the "The Structure of Introductions" diagram above and the model paragraph to guide you.

Unit 10
Sustainable Design

READING SECTION

Singapore: The Sustainable City 11

Since its independence in 1965, Singapore has become famous as a thriving, cosmopolitan, economic powerhouse. A small island country, poor in natural resources, Singapore has transformed from a country where more than half the country lived in slums to having the highest GDP per capita in Asia and among the highest
5 levels of education in the world. Having achieved economic development, Singapore now aims to be an international model of urban sustainability.

Singapore is one of the most highly urbanized countries in the world, and sustainability is a challenge. More than 5 million people live in an area one third the size of Tokyo. Eighty percent of Singapore residents live in high-rise buildings. And yet, the government of Singapore, working alongside businesses and
10 residents, is transforming the city. Singapore has developed goals of having "lush environments, renewable energy and future sustainability." Much of the change in policy can be attributed to Ms. Cheong Koon Hean, the first woman to lead Singapore's urban development agency.

One of Singapore's strategies is bringing back nature to the city. Because land is limited, skyline greenery has become increasingly important in Singapore. Skyline greenery includes covering rooftops with
15 grass, building rooftop gardens with public access and installing vertical greenery—plants that grow up walls and other vertical surfaces. More greenery is believed to improve air quality, cool the city and improve quality of life generally. Bringing nature back includes making green corridors to increase plant and animal biodiversity. In the 1980s Singapore's green cover was about 36%. Now, it is around 47%. With government subsidies and support from business and residents, Singapore is aiming to further increase this amount.
20 Other strategies that Singapore is pursuing are resource sustainability and renewable energy. Singapore has taken the approach that environmental protection can co-exist with economic development. Singapore has few natural resources, including water. In the past, it has relied on neighboring Malaysia for most of its water supply; however, by the year 2060, Singapore aims to supply 85% of its water needs through recycled water and desalination of seawater. Rooftop and vertical gardens are now expanding Singapore's ability to
25 grow its own food; currently, 90 percent of Singapore's food is imported. In terms of energy self-sufficiency, lack of resources means that Singapore has few options. The government is investing heavily in ways to reduce energy consumption as well as develop alternative energies.

An interesting aspect of Singapore's push to become a green city is that the government is involving the citizens. Sustainability is not just efficient use of resources; it is also building a resilient community that can
30 withstand major changes brought by globalization and climate change. The plans aim to build resilience by improving facilities and services for people. Ways to achieve this include creating jobs within the community, providing community space and developing well-connected transport. In order to implement the plan effectively, the people need to be involved. People are becoming active by looking after common gardens, reducing waste, and keeping spaces clean. An ideal model of sustainability is not just about
35 imposing policies, it is about building community resilience and rethinking the way the society operates.
(522 words)

Vocabulary

thriving（繁栄している）, cosmopolitan（国際的な）, powerhouse（原動力になる国）, transformed（生まれ変わった）, GDP（国内総生産 / Gross Domestic Product）, per capita（一人当たり）, aim to（〜を目指す）, urban sustainability（都市持続性）, urbanized country（都市化された国）, one third（三分の一、1/3）, lush environment（緑豊かな環境）, renewable energy（再生可能エネルギー）, attributed to（〜に起因する）, skyline greenery（地平線のように広がる緑樹）, corridor（廊下、通路）, biodiversity（生物多様性）, co-exist（共存する）, rely on（〜に依存する）, desalination（脱塩／淡水化）, in terms of（〜に関して）, self-sufficiency（自給自足）, alternative energy（代替エネルギー）, resilient community（強靭なコミュニティー）, withstand（耐える）, implement（実行する、適用する）, involve（巻き込む）

Vocabulary Exercise

1 Find the closest meaning from a-e for each word below.

1. powerhouse (   )
2. aim to (   )
3. corridors (   )
4. cosmopolitan (   )
5. withstand (   )

a. passageways
b. having a goal
c. put up with, confront with resistance
d. international
e. something energetic / strong

2 Write the most appropriate word to complete the sentences. (You may need to change the form of the word.) There are some words in the box that you don't use.

1. Vertical gardens are one way to (   ) a policy to green the city.
2. Singapore (   ) on imports because it has few natural resources.
3. Singapore has (   ) into a country where education and income levels are very high.
4. In order to create a sustainable city, it's necessary to (   ) ordinary people and get them to participate in improving the city.

| rely | consumption | implement | thriving | transform | involve |

Comprehension Questions

1 Write T if the statement is true according to the text and F if it is not true

1. Singapore depends on other countries for most of its natural resources. (   )
2. At the time of independence, most people in Singapore were wealthy. (   )
3. Economic development and sustainability can occur at the same time. (   )
4. 85% of Singapore's drinking water comes from desalinating seawater. (   )
5. Jobs and transportation are included in Singapore's sustainability plans. (   )

2 Write an answer to each question below.

1. What two examples are given to show that Singapore has become a developed country?

   _____

2. What are three benefits of having more greenery in a city?

   _____

3. What two strategies is Singapore using to overcome the lack of energy sources?

   _____

4. In addition to using resources well, what else does Singapore considered important for sustainability?

   _____

WRITING SECTION

WRITING FOCUS: Body paragraphs

In the body paragraphs of your essay, you give the reasons which support your thesis statement. Each paragraph of the body has a **topic sentence** and **supporting sentences**. These topic sentences are the reasons which you gave to support your thesis statement in the introduction. The supporting sentences provide details using explanations, examples, statistics, or expert's opinions (see page 16). Each supporting sentence must support the topic sentence. The purpose of supporting sentences is to show why the topic sentence is true.

The Structure of Body Paragraphs

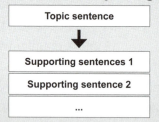

A good way to think of supporting sentences is to brainstorm. One way of doing this is to change the topic sentence into a question. The answers to the topic questions are the supporting sentences of your body paragraphs. For example, suppose that your topic sentence is the following:

Topic Sentence: *Parks are a good place for people to gather in their communities.*
This can be turned into a topic question.
Topic question: *Why are parks good places for people to gather in their communities?*

EXERCISE

1 Brainstorm for Reasons (Use a separate sheet of paper for this exercise.)

1. Turn each of your topic sentences into topic questions.

2. For each topic question, brainstorm as many answers as you can. Answers may be explanations, examples, statistics, an expert's opinion, or other information sentences.

3. Get into pairs. Explain to your partner why the answers to the topic questions you wrote down are good ones. After you discuss them, give feedback to your partner by answering the following questions.
    • Which reasons do you think are the best for answering the topic questions?
    • Why do you think they are the best?
    • How could they be improved?
    • Does each one have clear topic and topic focus?

4. Rewrite the answers so that they are in full-sentence form.

5. These are now the supporting sentences of the topic sentence of each body paragraph.

When you write body paragraphs, make sure to include a transition in the topic sentence of each paragraph. You also need to include transitions in your supporting sentences. You will find a list of transition phrases below.

- One way/reason that _____ is …
- Another way/reason that _____ is …
- First, …/Second, …/Third, …/Lastly, …
- Furthermore, …/Moreover,…/Equally important, ...
- In addition, …/Also, …/Besides, …
- Besides _____, ….In addition to _____, …

2 Read the model paragraph and follow the directions below.

A MODEL BODY PARAGRAPH

One reason that every town should have a big park is that parks are good places for people to gather in their community. First, parks are safe. Kondo, Hohl., Han, and Branas (2016) pointed out that parks are safer places to gather than land that is not being used. So, the more park land there is, the more safe places there are for people in the community to gather. Second, parks are places where we can meet new people in the community. For example, farmers markets, barbecues, and concerts are all great places to meet new people, and big parks provide the space and atmosphere for these events. (108 words)

Reference
    Kondo, M., Hohl, B., Han, S., & Branas, C. (2016). Effects of greening and community reuse of vacant lots on crime. *Urban Studies*, 53(15), 3279-3295.

1. Circle all the transition phrases used in the model paragraph.

2. Among the transition phrases you circled, write the ones which are used for the topic sentence or the supporting sentences.

   Topic Sentence: _____

   Supporting Sentence 1: _____

   Supporting Sentence 2: _____

3 Write the Body Paragraphs of Your Essay (Homework assignment)

Using your topic sentences and supporting sentences, write three body paragraphs to your essay on a separate sheet of paper. You may want to refer to both your outline and the model body paragraph to get ideas for organizing your writing.

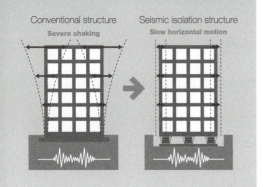

Unit 11
Natural Hazards

READING SECTION

Seismic Design and Technology at NMWA

In seismically active countries like Japan, structural engineers need to consider the effect of earthquakes. Good planning and up-to-date technology reduce damage and save lives. There are various structural design methods for limiting the effect of earthquakes on buildings. As technology improves, earthquake mitigation techniques also improve. We can see this in the construction and retrofitting of the National Museum of Western Art (NMWA) in Ueno, Tokyo.

When it was constructed in 1959, the NMWA utilized the basic method of reducing the impact of an earthquake on a building, i.e., making the building rigid so that it can withstand the force of an earthquake. The building, designed by Le Corbusier, posed a challenge because one of the signature features of the building, pilotis, is structurally vulnerable to collapse in an earthquake. Pilotis are a series of columns that lift a building off the ground. The greatest vertical load on each column occurs at the base. This means that during an earthquake, the columns have to be rigid enough to withstand significant horizontal shaking (or lateral force). To do this, the engineers adapted Le Corbusier's plan by increasing the size of beams and pilotis. However, making the building rigid doesn't reduce the movement induced to the building during an earthquake; once the structure is damaged, it has no resilience to further damage and the building may collapse. Despite the adaptations to Le Corbusier's plans, the NMWA was still very vulnerable to a large earthquake. In the event of an earthquake both the building and the valuable art collection inside could be destroyed.

In 1981, new building regulations with stricter seismic requirements were introduced for new buildings in Japan. Under the new rules, the NMWA had less than half of the seismic resistance that was required. As new technologies for seismic resistance developed, the NMWA began to look at other ways to reduce the risk of damage. In 1998, the NMWA was the first building in Japan to retrofit a seismic isolator; a new foundation, made of layers of rubber sheets, was inserted between the ground and the footings, including those of the pilotis. This means that when an earthquake occurs, the isolator dramatically reduces the force of an earthquake on the building. The horizontal movement of the earth is mitigated, so the building is much less likely to be damaged. Safety has been improved without losing the features of Le Corbusier's design. Seismic isolation can also be found under Rodin's statue of the Gates of Hell in the grounds of the NMWA. In this case though, the seismic isolation technique uses rollers instead of rubber.

The case of the NMWA shows how structural engineers can reduce the risk of damage from an earthquake both in the design stage and after completion. (460 words)

Vocabulary

seismically active country (地震活動が活発な国), up-to-date (最新の), mitigation (軽減), construction (工事), retrofit (新部品、装置などを追加導入する、改造する、改築する), utilize (利用する), rigid (頑丈な、剛性の), withstand (耐える), pose a challenge (問題を提起する), signature feature (最大の特徴), vulnerable (脆弱な), collapse (崩壊する、崩れる), column (柱), vertical (垂直の), load (荷重), significant (著しい), lateral force (横方向の力、水平力), beam (梁), induce (引き起こされる), resilience (弾性、弾力), adaptation (改造), seismic isolator (免震装置), dramatically (劇的に), Rodin's statue (ロダンの彫刻), Gates of Hell (地獄の門), completion (完成)

Unit 11

Vocabulary Exercise

1 Find the closest meaning from a-e for each word below.

1. mitigation (   )
2. rigid (   )
3. vulnerable (   )
4. adaptation (   )
5. utilize (   )

a. use
b. the process of changing to suit different conditions
c. at risk of being damaged or hurt
d. strong and doesn't break easily
e. reduction of effect

2 Write the most appropriate word to complete the sentences. (You may need to change the form of the word.) There are some words in the box that you don't use.

1. The building has been built so that it can (   ) an earthquake that is M9.
2. I felt (   ) movements first when the earthquake occurred.
3. Buildings without seismic reinforcement are more likely to (   ) in an earthquake.
4. Improvements in technology have meant vulnerable buildings can be (   ) with seismic isolators.

| load | induce | vertical | withstand | collapse | retrofit |

Comprehension Questions

1 Write T if the statement is true according to the text and F if it is not true.

1. A country that is seismically active has earthquakes. (   )
2. Le Corbusier changed the columns so they would withstand the force of an earthquake. (   )
3. Making a building rigid is the best technique to prevent earthquake damage. (   )
4. The 1959 building code tightened earthquake regulations. (   )

2 Write an answer to each question below.

1. What feature of Le Corbusier's architecture is likely to be damaged in an earthquake? _____

2. Where does the greatest vertical load occur on the pilotis?
   _____

3. What action did the NMWA take to reduce the risk of earthquake damage?
   _____

4. In addition to a rubber layer, what other method of seismic isolation can be found at the NMWA? _____

47

WRITING SECTION

WRITING FOCUS: Writing a concluding paragraph

The final paragraph of your essay is called a concluding paragraph. The purpose of a conclusion is to summarize the main points of your essay. When writing a concluding paragraph, it is a good idea to paraphrase the thesis statement. Then, it is often a good idea to summarize the main reasons you gave in support of your thesis statement (your topic sentences). Your concluding paragraph should not include any new information. You may want to end your concluding paragraph with a comment on your thesis statement. A concluding comment often states the importance of the topic which you have chosen. A concluding comment is meant to make the reader remember the essay.

The Structure of a Conclusion

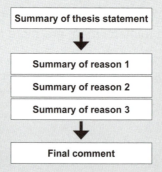

You should signal to the reader that you are beginning your concluding paragraph in the first sentence of the concluding paragraph. The following is a list of phrases which are used to signal a concluding paragraph:

- In sum,
- To conclude,
- To sum up,
- In conclusion,
- In summary,
- In brief,
- To summarize,

EXERCISE

1 Read the model paragraph and follow the directions below.

A MODEL CONCLUSION PARAGRAPH

(A) In sum, every community needs a big park. (B) A variety of reasons support this claim. (C) Since parks are places for grass, trees, and plants, the air quality of towns with big parks improves. (D) Moreover, parks provide both open space and a natural cushion of grass which stops injuries. (E) These points make parks an ideal place to exercise, which supports the health of the residents of any town. (F) Finally, parks are safe places for people in the community to gather for various events. (G) This increases the feeling of community and trust between community members. (H) Parks increase physical, mental, environmental, and social wellbeing, and their importance must not be ignored.

(116 words)

Match the sentence types on the right with the letters on the left. You may need to match more than one letter on the left with a single sentence on the right.

(A) ·
(B) ·   · Summary of Reason 3
(C) ·   · Concluding Comment
(D) ·   · Summary of Reason 2
(E) ·   · Summary of Thesis Statement
(F) ·   · Summary of Reason 1
(G) ·   · None of the Above
(H) ·

2 Concluding Comment

Write a few possible concluding comments for your concluding paragraph. One way to write a concluding comment is to emphasize the importance of your topic. Let us continue to use the following thesis statement:

Every town in Japan should have a big park.

By emphasizing the importance of this thesis statement, you can make a concluding comment that the reader will remember:

Big parks are an essential part of any town or city, and the lives of all people in a town or city with big parks are improved by them.

Another way to write a concluding comment is to describe the positive effects that action based on your thesis statement can have.

Working to build more big parks in your city can both improve your life and the lives of future generations.

Now, try to write your own concluding comment for your thesis statement.

3 Write the Conclusion of Your Essay

Write your own conclusion on a separate sheet of paper. Keep the structure of conclusions in mind when you are writing. You may want to use the "The Structure of Conclusions" diagram above and the model paragraph to guide you.

Unit 12
Urban Design

READING SECTION

Planned Cities

Throughout history, many capital cities have grown organically. They start as small settlements, often near rivers or harbors or important points on a trade route. Over time, they expand and gain regional importance as the political and often commercial center. In a few countries, though, the capital cities have been planned. In Japan, for example, the ancient capitals of Kyoto and Nara were both planned. They were based on the city design of Chang'an, now known as Xi'an, in China. The location of both was based on the principles of feng shui: there was a river in the east, a wide street in the west, a plain or a pond in the south and a hill in the north. In New World countries which are products of colonization, there are several planned capitals: Canberra, Australia and Brasilia, Brazil are two well-known examples.

When choosing the location of the capital, practical matters such as climate, access to water and energy need to be considered. However, compromise may be necessary in choosing a location to ensure that the city is seen to be representing all people. This occurred with Canberra, Australia. Canberra was built as a compromise location halfway between the two biggest cities in Australia at the time, Sydney and Melbourne. Neither Sydney nor Melbourne wanted the other to become the capital. As a result, in 1908, Canberra, which is approximately halfway between the two cities, was agreed upon as the site for the capital. In the case of Brasilia, it was built in 1961 as an alternative to the existing capital, Rio de Janeiro. Rio was overcrowded, far away from most of the country, and its geographical location made expansion difficult.

In addition to practical reasons, a planned capital tends to have philosophical and symbolic dimensions, such as expressing national identity or creating national unity. In the case of Australia, the prominent locations of the Parliament and the War Memorial symbolize national unity. In the case of Brasilia, relocating the Brazilian capital to the center of the country was a way to break from the colonial past and create a vision for the future. Brazil could strengthen its identity as an independent, forward-looking country. Brasilia was designed by two eminent Brazilians: Lucio Costa, who made the city plan, and Oscar Niemeyer, who designed many of the landmark buildings. Their success is shown by the fact that Brasilia is the only World Heritage city designed in the 20th century.

A characteristic of planned cities is that the buildings tend to come before the people. Despite impressive architecture, Canberra and Brasilia are often criticized for being artificial and lacking an organically developed cultural life. Both cities have also been criticized for relying on cars rather than having a pedestrian culture. In both cases, this is caused partly by zoning which separates the commercial and residential areas of the cities. However, as time has progressed, residents have formed communities and the cities have gradually developed a human face on top of the idealistic plans. Both cities have begun to evolve their own organic culture. Analysis of planned cities provides a good opportunity for us to reflect on what it is that makes a city and gives it life. (535 words)

Vocabulary

organically（有機的に）, settlements（集落）, regional（地域の）, commercial（商業の）, Chang'an（長安）, Xi'an（西安）, feng shui（風水）, New World（新世界；西半球、オーストラリア、ニュージーランドを含む場合もある）, colonization（植民地化；入植）, practical matter（実際の事柄）, compromise（妥協（する））, ensure（…を確かにする）, approximately（おおよそ）, alternative（代替手段［案］）, overcrowded（人口過密）, philosophical（哲学的）, symbolic（象徴的）, dimension（側面）, Parliament（議会）, strengthen（強化する）, eminent（著名な）, despite（…にもかかわらず）, artificial（人工的）, criticized（批判される）, pedestrian culture（歩行者文化）, evolve（進化する）, reflect（反映する、顧みる）

Unit 12

Vocabulary Exercise

1 Find the closest meaning from a-e for each word below.

1. practical ( )
2. approximately ( )
3. organic ( )
4. evolve ( )
5. eminent ( )

a. almost, not exactly
b. unplanned, happening in a natural way
c. famous and important (person)
d. based on real things rather than ideals
e. change gradually over a period of time

2 Write the most appropriate word to complete the sentences. (You may need to change the form of the word.) There are some words in the box that you don't use.

1. The government tried to (   ) that all citizens felt represented by it.
2. Public transport is usually a more ecological (   ) to private cars.
3. Neither of them could convince the other of their opinion so they had to (   ) and find a solution they could both accept.
4. Even if a planned city begins with a feeling that it is (   ), it should develop its own culture over time.

| artificial | ensure | alternative | compromise | despite | symbolic |

Comprehension Questions

1 Write T if the statement is true according to the text and F if it is not true.

1. Canberra and Brasilia were located through principles of feng shui. ( )
2. Canberra was a popular choice as the capital of Australia. ( )
3. Rio de Janeiro was a suitable location for a national capital. ( )
4. Brasilia was intended as a symbol of national unity. ( )
5. Organic cultural life has developed in both Brasilia and Canberra. ( )

2 Write an answer to each question below.

1. Which city provided a model for Nara and Kyoto?

   _____

2. Why was the location of Canberra chosen?

   _____

3. How has the success of Brasilia been recognized?

   _____

4. What three things have Brasilia and Canberra both been criticized for?

   _____

WRITING SECTION

WRITING FOCUS: Title, Revising, and Proofreading Your Essay

> The title is the "face" of your essay. A good title both gives information about the content of your essay and makes people want to read it. Except for most prepositions (of, at, for, etc.) and conjunctions ("and", "but", "or"), the first letter of each word of a title should a capital letter. The exception is prepositions with five or more letters (e.g. through), which should start with a capital letter. Keep in mind that these rules are for APA format. Other writing styles, such as MLA and Chicago style, may have different rules for titles.

EXERCISE

1 Write the Title of Your Essay

Consider the main point of your essay and write its title. If you can make a title that gets the attention of readers, that is even better.

Title: _____

The final step of essay writing is to improve your essay through **revising** and **proofreading**. When you revise, you focus on larger aspects of your essay, such as content and organization. When you proofread, you focus on smaller aspects of your writing, such as format, grammar, and punctuation. It is easier to revise and proofread when you have a checklist like the following:

		CONTENT & ORGANIZATION (REVISING)	
1		Does the essay have a title, an introduction, a body, and a conclusion?	
2	Introduction	Does the attention getter get the reader's attention?	
3		Is the thesis statement clear and does it have a topic and topic focus?	
4	Body	Does each body paragraph support the thesis?	
5		Does each body paragraph have a topic sentence that supports the thesis statement?	
6		Does each body paragraph have well developed supporting sentences (explanations, examples...)?	
7		Does each body paragraph contain one main idea?	
8		Are the supporting sentences logically connected to their topic sentences?	
9	Conclusion	Does the conclusion summarize the thesis statement and the topic sentences of the body paragraphs?	
10		Does the conclusion contain a concluding comment?	

FORMAT, GRAMMAR AND PUNCTUATION (PROOFREADING)		
11	Is each paragraph indented?	
12	Are margins kept on both sides? (If using word processor, use justification (両端揃え), or leave about an inch space on both sides if handwriting.)	
13	Is there a period, question mark, or exclamation point at the end of each sentence?	
14	Are capital letters used where necessary?	
15	Does each sentence have a subject and a verb and express a complete thought?	
16	Does each verb agree with its subject?	
17	Are verb tenses correct?	
18	Are commas used correctly?	

2 Revise and Proofread Your Essay

1. Using the checklist above, revise and proofread your essay.

2. Get in pairs. Exchange your essay with your partner and revise and proofread your partner's essay using the checklist. Then, give your partner comments by answering the following questions:
    A. What are the best parts of the essay?
    B. Which parts of the essay can be improved?
    C. How can the parts in B be improved?

3. According to the comments you got from your partner, revise and proofread your essay again.

Reference & Further reading

Unit 1: Introduction
Pritzerprize: https://www.pritzkerprize.com/
Architects Journal: https://www.architectsjournal.co.uk/
Arch Daily: https://www.archdaily.com/
Dezeen: https://www.dezeen.com/
Design Boom: https://www.designboom.com/

Unit 2: Planning
Sim Lab: http://www.sim.arc.shibaura-it.ac.jp/en/tsukishima/
Hideaki Shimura, Tsukishima saihakkengaku. Machizukuri shiten de tanoshimu rekishi to mirai [The rediscovery of Tsukishima: History and future as seen from an urban development viewpoint] (Tokyo: Anika, 2013)

Unit 3: Floor Plan
Praprika: http://yalepaprika.com/danchi-dreams/
Interaction Green: http://www.interactiongreen.com/muji-x-ur/
New York Times: https://www.nytimes.com/2017/11/30/world/asia/japan-lonely-deaths-the-end.html
Quartz:https://qz.com/490730/muji-is-redesigning-tokyos-cheap-estate-housing-as-a-hip-lifestyle-choice/
The Japan Times: https://www.japantimes.co.jp/community/2003/01/19/general/the-danchi-and-postwar-society

Unit 4: Building Structure
Sagrada Familia Official site: http://www.sagradafamilia.org/en/
+ Maths Magazine: https://plus.maths.org/content/matjhs-minute-catenary
Criticalista: https://criticalista.com/2012/08/16/gaudis-hanging-chain-models-parametric-design-avant-la-lettre/
BBC: http://www.bbc.com/earth/story/20150913-nine-incredible-buildings-inspired-by-nature

Unit 5: Kitchens
The Telegraph: https://www.telegraph.co.uk/women/womens-life/9721147/Women-spend-half-as-much-time-on-housework-today-compared-to-1960s.html
Architectural Digest: https://www.architecturaldigest.com/story/kitchen-design-style-through-the-years
CY Lee architects: https://www.cylee.com/project/Taipei-101
BBC: http://www.bbc.com/earth/story/20150913-nine-incredible-buildings-inspired-by-nature

Unit 6: Living Rooms
Arch Daily: https://www.archdaily.com/873077/ad-classics-red-house-arts-crafts-william-morris-philip-webb
The Guardian: https://www.theguardian.com/artanddesign/2003/jul/26/art.architecture
Academia: http://www.academia.edu/34770046/Horace_Walpole_s_Strawberry_Hill_House_and_William_Morris_s_Red_House_Idealisation_of_Gothic_as_Reflection_of_New_Modernity_
Victoria and Albert Museum: https://www.vam.ac.uk/articles/arts-and-crafts-an-introduction
Khan Academy: https://www.khanacademy.org/humanities/becoming-modern/victorian-art-architecture/pre-raphaelites/a/william-morris-and-philip-webb-red-house

Unit 7: Design Styles
Health and Safety Executive: http://www.hse.gov.uk/temperature/thermal/factors.htm
Design Buildings Wiki: https://www.designingbuildings.co.uk/wiki/Thermal_comfort_in_buildings

Unit 8: Scales and Dimensions

Icon: https://www.iconeye.com/opinion/icon-of-the-month/item/3815-modulor-man-by-le-corbusier
European Architectural History Network: https://journal.eahn.org/articles/10.5334/ah.by/
There's something about phi - Chapter 20 - Le Corbusier and the Modulor
https://www.youtube.com/watch?v=JGMaND8tQoM
The Official website of the Chandigarh Administration. http://chandigarh.gov.in/knowchd_edict.htm
Architectural Institute of Japan: http://touron.aij.or.jp/2016/03/1056

Unit 9: Colors and Materials

Architect: https://archinect.com/features/article/53292622/color-in-architecture-more-than-just-decoration
Wonderful Colors: http://www.wonderfulcolors.org/blog/birren-color-theory/
TMD Studio: https://medium.com/studiotmd/the-perception-of-color-in-architecture-cf360676776c
Pantone: https://www.pantone.com/color-psychology-how-does-color-affect-us

Unit 10: Sustainable Design

CNN: https://edition.cnn.com/travel/article/singapore-greenest-city/index.html
National Geographic: https://www.nationalgeographic.com/environment/urban-expeditions/green-buildings/green-urban-landscape-cities-Singapore/
Ministry of the Environment and Water Resources and Ministry of National Development: https://www.mewr.gov.sg/ssb/home

Unit 11: Natural Hazards

Ministry of Land, Infrastructure, Transport and Tourism: http://www.mlit.go.jp/common/001153144.pdf
Takenaka: http://www.takenaka.co.jp/news/pr9903/m9903_04.htm
Khan Academy: https://www.khanacademy.org/partner-content/getty-museum/getty-art-conservation/v/protecting-art-earthquake-seismic-isolator-technology

Unit 12: Urban Design

The Guardian City Building Crash Course: https://citybuildingcrashcourse.wordpress.com/2014/08/27/city-structure-models/
Kyoto City Official Website: http://www.city.kyoto.lg.jp/tokei/cmsfiles/contents/0000057/57538/2shou.pdf
The Guardian: https://www.theguardian.com/cities/2015/jun/30/how-build-city-step-by-step-diy-guide
The Guardian: https://www.theguardian.com/cities/2016/apr/07/story-cities-17-canberra-capital-australia-walter-griffin-ideal-city
National Archives of Australia: http://www.naa.gov.au/collection/fact-sheets/fs95.aspx
UNESCO Brasilia: https://whc.unesco.org/en/list/445

ホートン広瀬恵美子 **(Horton Hirose, Emiko)**：芝浦工業大学建築学部・共通教養外国語科目（教授）
    BA（英語教授法 Teaching English as a Second Language）Hawaii Pacific University; MA（言語学 Linguistics）University of Hawaii

スミス 藤島 セシリア **(Cecilia Smith Fujishima)**：白百合女子大学（講師）
    BA (History), Sydney University; MA (Global Studies), 上智大学

恒安（堀川）眞佐 **(Tsuneyasu Horikawa, Masa)**：国際基督教大学（特任講師）
    2019年4月より芝浦工業大学建築学部共通教養外国語科目（准教授）

神谷英子 **(Kamiya, Hanako)**：日建設計コンストラクション・マネジメント株式会社；芝浦工業大学建築学部（非常勤講師）
    BS（建築), 芝浦工業大学；MA (Architecture), Pratt Institute Graduate School of Architecture and Urban Design（米国）；米国および他の海外で9年間建設業務に従事.

パネル ジャスティン **(Justin Pannell)**：ハワイ大学マノア校 ESL 講師
    MA（哲学），Syracuse University; MA（英語教授法 Teaching English to Speakers of Other Languages），Hawaii Pacific University

ホートン広瀬レイナ **(Horton Hirose, Reina)**：English Language Centers Honolulu 講師；UH Manoa Outreach College 講師
    BA（政治学），早稲田大学；MA（英語教授法 Teaching English to Speakers of Other Languages），Hawaii Pacific University

┌─────────────────────────────────────┐
│ 著作権法上、無断複写・複製は禁じられています。 │
└─────────────────────────────────────┘

Basic English for Architecture —Reading & Writing—	[B-873]
建築を学ぶ人のための総合英語 ― リーディング＆ライティング ―	

1	刷	2019年 3月28日	
2	刷	2023年 8月31日	

著　者	ホートン 広瀬 恵美子	Emiko Hirose Horton
	スミス 藤島 セシリア	Cecilia Smith Fujishima
	恒安（堀川）眞佐	Tsuneyasu Horikawa, Masa
	神谷　英子	Hanako Kamiya
	パネル ジャスティン	Justin Pannell
	ホートン 広瀬 レイナ	Reina Hirose Horton

発行者　　南雲　一範　　Kazunori Nagumo
発行所　　株式会社　南雲堂
　　　　　〒162-0801　東京都新宿区山吹町361
　　　　　NAN'UN-DO Co., Ltd.
　　　　　361 Yamabuki-cho, Shinjuku-ku, Tokyo 162-0801, Japan
　　　　　振替口座：00160-0-46863
　　　　　TEL: 03-3268-2311（営業部：学校関係）
　　　　　　　 03-3268-2384（営業部：書店関係）
　　　　　　　 03-3268-2387（編集部）
　　　　　FAX: 03-3269-2486

編集者	加藤　敦
製　版	橋本　佳子
装　丁	銀月堂
検　印	省　略
コード	ISBN978-4-523-17873-6　C0082

Printed in Japan

E-mail　nanundo@post.email.ne.jp
URL　　https://www.nanun-do.co.jp/

DESIGN ENGLISH
クリエイターのための闘う英語

高山靖子　亀井暁子　高瀬奈美　服部守悦　峯郁郎
Edward Sarich　Gary McLeod　Jack Ryan　Mark Sheehan　著

デザインの現場における経験をもとに
デザインを検討するときに使う言葉と
英会話のポイントをまとめた実践に
役立つ一冊！

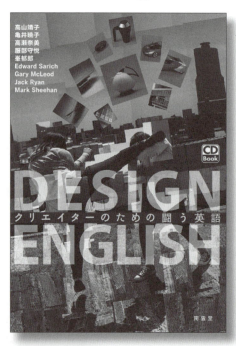

定価（本体 2,800 円＋税）
A5 判 216 ページ＋別冊 86 ページ
ISBN978-4-523-26543-6　C0082

巻末にはデザイン検討
の際に使用される、
辞書では調べにくい
語彙、表現を掲載

南雲堂

〒 162-0801 東京都新宿区山吹町 361　　TEL 03-3268-2384　FAX 03-3260-5425